MY LEADING WHILE FEMALE JOURNEY

MY *LEADING WHILE FEMALE* JOURNEY
A Guided Reflective Journal

Trudy T. Arriaga
Stacie L. Stanley
Delores B. Lindsey

Foreword by Julie A. Vitale

FOR INFORMATION

Corwin

A SAGE Company

2455 Teller Road

Thousand Oaks, California 91320

(800) 233-9936

www.corwin.com

SAGE Publications Ltd.

1 Oliver's Yard

55 City Road

London EC1Y 1SP

United Kingdom

SAGE Publications India Pvt. Ltd.

B 1/I 1 Mohan Cooperative Industrial Area

Mathura Road, New Delhi 110 044

India

SAGE Publications Asia-Pacific Pte. Ltd.

18 Cross Street #10-10/11/12

China Square Central

Singapore 048423

President: Mike Soules

Vice President and Editorial
   Director: Monica Eckman

Program Director and Publisher: Dan Alpert

Acquisitions Editor: Megan Bedell

Associate Content Development
   Editor: Mia Rodriguez

Editorial Intern: Ricardo Ramirez

Project Editor: Amy Schroller

Copy Editor: Erin Livingston

Typesetter: Hurix Digital

Proofreader: Dennis Webb

Cover Designer: Scott Van Atta

Marketing Manager: Melissa Duclos

Library of Congress Control Number: 2022916729

This book is printed on acid-free paper.

22 23 24 25 26 10 9 8 7 6 5 4 3 2 1

DISCLAIMER: This book may direct you to access third-party content via web links, QR codes, or other scannable technologies, which are provided for your reference by the author(s). Corwin makes no guarantee that such third-party content will be available for your use and encourages you to review the terms and conditions of such third-party content. Corwin takes no responsibility and assumes no liability for your use of any third-party content, nor does Corwin approve, sponsor, endorse, verify, or certify such third-party content.

CONTENTS

FOREWORD

What a privilege to read a book that speaks to me as a female leader. That was my first reaction when I read *Leading While Female*. This follow-up companion, *My Leading While Female Journey: A Guided Reflective Journal*, now provides me with the opportunity to truly think about myself and my career within the context of additional powerful stories written by women, for women. Feeling the support and encouragement of women who have walked before me and alongside me gave me the overwhelming sense of generational support. I see myself in every story as women of various ages, ethnicities, and sexual orientations are represented in this reflective journal.

The reflection component is the portion of the book that challenged me and forced me to hit pause and slow down my ever-racing mind. When we really think about how we get in our own way, or as quoted in the book from Brené Brown (2018), "your stormy first draft, the story you are making up about yourself," we realize only we have the power to shift our thinking. We do not have to accept things as they are; we do not have to function in the "old boy network." We, as women, have the influence and intelligence to create new structures and new realities for the workplace. That is the thought I had at the end of working my way through the various structures for reflection as provided in this reflective journal. I invite you to engage with these stories as an exercise in your own personal empowerment and see what new reality you create for yourself!

—Julie A. Vitale
Superintendent
Oceanside Unified School District

ACKNOWLEDGMENTS

We, the authors, greatly appreciate the expertise and continuous support of the Corwin team: Dan Alpert, senior acquisitions editor; Lucas Schleicher, senior content development editor; Mia Rodriguez, content development editor; and Scott Van Atta, senior graphic designer.

Each team member shared their time, ideas, and encouragement with us. For that, we are most grateful.

We acknowledge female leaders who took the time to share their stories with us so that we could share them with our readers. Their stories became prompts for reflections and Stormy First Drafts for other leaders. Thanks to our Facebook group members who responded to our survey that yielded data to inform this guided reflection journal. We appreciate our families, who stood beside us as we harnessed our dream to celebrate, inspire, and equip future female/women executives in education. Thank you to all the women who have and will fix a woman's crooked crown without announcing it. When one of us does better, we all do better.

ABOUT THE AUTHORS

Trudy T. Arriaga serves as the associate dean of equity and outreach in the graduate school of education at California Lutheran University in Thousand Oaks, CA. She is co-author of *Leading While Female: A Culturally Proficient Response for Gender Equity* and *Opening Doors: An Implementation Template for Cultural Proficiency*. Dr. Arriaga served the Ventura Unified School District for 14 years as the first female superintendent. She began her career as a bilingual paraeducator and enjoyed 40 years of service in education as a teacher, assistant principal, principal, director, and superintendent. Trudy retired as superintendent in July 2015 and was honored by the naming of the VUSD District Office as The VUSD Trudy Tuttle Arriaga Education Service Center. It has been her privilege to assist educational institutions and organizations throughout the United States through keynote speeches, workshops, leadership and equity institutes, and professional development to align the actions of the organization with their stated values and principles in their effort to build a culturally proficient and inclusive organization for each and every one. Trudy and her husband, Raymundo, are enjoying this grand chapter of life with their grandchildren.

Stacie L. Stanley serves as the superintendent of Edina Public Schools. Dr. Stanley has served in a variety of education roles, including classroom teacher; elementary school principal; math specialist; curriculum and staff development specialist; director of achievement equity; director of curriculum, assessment, and instruction; and associate superintendent. Stacie is a senior training associate at the Center for Culturally Proficient Educational Practice and the co-author of *Leading While Female: A Culturally Proficient Response for Gender Equity*. She is a fierce advocate for ensuring women are positioned to move into executive leadership roles—including a special focus on women of color. She earned a doctorate from Bethel University in Saint Paul, Minnesota, where she researched the impact of intercultural development on K–6 administrative leadership practice. Stacie is also an adjunct faculty member in the Bethel University doctoral program in Minnesota and a member of the Hamline School of Education advisory board. She lives with her husband and enjoys being an empty nester, taking long walks, and spending time with their grandchildren.

Delores B. Lindsey retired as assistant professor of educational leadership at California State University San Marcos; however, she has not retired from the education profession. Dr. Lindsey's primary focus is developing culturally proficient leaders. She helps educational leaders examine their organizations' policies and practices and their individual beliefs and values about cross-cultural communication. Her message to her audiences focuses on viewing, creating, and managing socially just educational practices, culturally proficient leadership practice, and diversity as an asset to be nurtured. Her favorite reflective question is *Are we who we say we are?* Delores and her husband, Randall (her favorite SAGE/Corwin author), continue to co-write about the application of the four tools of Cultural Proficiency. Her most recent publication, which is on the bestseller list from Corwin, is *Leading While Female: A Culturally Proficient Response for Gender Equity,* with Trudy T. Arriaga and Stacie L. Stanley.

I, Trudy, dedicate this journal to my mother, Arlys Leone Tuttle. Equipped with 100 years of wisdom, she continues to generously give unconditional love, foot rubs, and a constant reminder that I am enough.

I, Stacie, dedicate this journal to my mother, Crola Arquila Slaughter Jones, who fostered a love for family, the desire to dream big, and an understanding of my God-given destiny.

I, Delores, dedicate this journal to the memory of my mother, Delores Holston Broom, who modeled grace under fire and taught me to believe in myself.

INTRODUCTION

The success of every woman should be the inspiration to another. We should raise each other up. Make sure you're very courageous: Be strong, be extremely kind, and above all, be humble.

—Serena Williams

PURPOSES OF THIS BOOK

Many of our readers of *Leading While Female: A Culturally Proficient Response for Gender Equity* (*LWF*) requested we write a book of reflective questions to accompany the book. We decided to write a companion journal to serve multiple purposes:

- As a workbook for leadership development in professional learning sessions

- As a personal reflection journal for leadership and professional growth

- As a workbook for professional learning communities focused on leadership growth and development

- As a guide for professional book studies

- As a bundle purchase with *Leading While Female* for a professional learning series for leaders

- As a companion book for university courses using *Leading While Female* as a main text for gender equity and leadership courses

We encourage readers to take advantage of the multiple purposes of this book. This book is designed for you to use individually as well as in your learning community. As with *LWF*, we invite female and male leaders to engage with the stories and reflective questions in this book. We also encourage you to invite emerging female leaders to join you on your cultural proficiency journey. *LWF* and this companion journal make an inspiring professional book study focused on gender equity, intersectionality, inclusion, overcoming barriers, utilizing support factors, sponsoring, and mentoring emerging leaders.

THEIR STORIES, REFLECTIONS, YOUR STORY

The current educational and corporate systems have suppressed women's leadership opportunities at all levels. As authors, advocates, and activists for gender equity, we continue to call out and confront systemic oppression of women and people of color in schools and districts. We also acknowledge male/female as a binary concept and yet a nonbinary spectrum of gender identities not limited to male or female identities exists. Some educational leaders who are members of the LGBTQIA+ (lesbian, gay, bisexual, transgender, queer/questioning, intersex, and asexual/aromantic/agender) community fear being their authentic selves in the workplace because of systemic barriers they face. Throughout this book, we use terms to support learning about all equity gaps. The following terms are defined using the lens of cultural proficiency:

Woman/Women/Female: The co-authors intentionally begin our list of terms with these three words. We are aware that the historical use of these terms has been perceived to mean *White* woman/women/female. With this in mind, the authors seek to clarify that when we use these terms, we mean *all* women. We also use the words *woman/women* and *female(s)* interchangeably throughout the book. We use the term *women of color* (WOC), specifically, when referring to other than White females. Although we use the terms *female* and *male* throughout the book, we are well aware of the limitations of our language in expressing the vast spectrum of gender identity. At the same time, we wish to acknowledge that the use of such terms is extremely reflective of a very real system of oppression.

Advocate: An individual who seeks to use personal positional power to intentionally lift the talents of women leaders and rally for opportunities that allow women to develop the skills needed to be successful in executive positions.

Coach: One who supports potential women leaders in surfacing consciousness around areas for growth and advancement. Leadership coaches serve to mediate the person being coached from emerging skills to mastering leader skills.

Gender equity: The fairness of treatment for men and women according to their respective needs. Equity may include equal treatment or treatment that is different but which is considered equivalent in terms of rights, benefits, obligations, and opportunities.

LGBTQIA+: An acronym for lesbian, gay, bisexual, transgender, queer/ questioning, intersex, asexual/aromantic/agender, and plus for other identities that are not straight and/or not cisgender.

Mentor: An experienced, well-seasoned veteran educational leader who imparts knowledge and personal experiences to women leaders who have been identified as candidates for future executive-level positions. Mentors consistently look for conferences and other professional learning opportunities to help position the female mentee for advancement. Mentors often support mentees through high-quality networking in organizations that provide interview skills to prepare female candidates.

Sponsor: One who actively uses positional power to partner with hiring authorities within their networks to advocate for the promotion of women leaders into high-leverage, decision-making positions.

Excerpted from *Leading While Female: A Culturally Proficient Response for Gender Equity*, pp. 11–14.

DESIGN OF THIS BOOK

This book is designed as a companion journal to *Leading While Female: A Culturally Proficient Response for Gender Equity*. Although this book will serve as a stand-alone journal, it is best enjoyed in tandem with the *LWF* chapters. Each chapter opens with a quote on which the reader will reflect and connect. Chapters 1–8 offer a leader's story aligned with each chapter title. A series of reflective questions follows the authentic leadership story. Chapter 9 presents a template for the reader to write a Stormy First Draft (SFD) followed by reflective questions.

Chapter 1: *Owning the Stories We Tell: We All Have a Story to Tell* reiterates the importance of leaders' narratives.

Chapter 2: *Cultural Proficiency: A Framework for Gender Equity* offers women a lens through which to examine the barriers to overcome in their personal and professional lives.

Chapter 3: *Confronting and Overcoming Barriers* reflects on the barriers found in systems of oppression and looks at the necessary steps for career development.

Chapter 4: *Moving Forward With Guiding Principles* requires leaders to examine core values, beliefs, and assumptions as support factors.

Chapter 5: *Understanding Feminism, Identity, and Intersectionality: Who Am I? Who Are We?* Understanding self and how the leader is perceived by others and understanding others are important parts of a leader's narrative and career path.

Chapter 6: *Men's Actions Allies, Advocates, and Mentors* reminds the reader that female leaders cannot do this work alone.

Chapter 7: *Next Steps?* focuses on planning and acting for the future.

Chapter 8: *Paying It Forward* comes when you still have something to offer the profession.

Chapter 9: *Template for Action: My Stormy First Draft (SFD)*.

 ► Leading While Female *means working together with female and male colleagues who are also grounded in values for equity . . . by sharing these barriers, support factors, and intentional actions, more women leaders today will interrupt current dominant narratives with their new stories of challenges and success.*

Leading While Female, p. 1

What might be some of your core values that will help you overcome barriers to working together?

_____

_____

_____

_____

_____

_____

_____

_____

In what ways do you see yourself *Leading While Female* using this definition?

_____

_____

_____

_____

_____

_____

_____

_____

We wish you well as you engage with these stories and reflective questions. Stay in touch. Our email addresses are

trudyarriaga73@gmail.com

staciestanley@gmail.com

deloreslindsey003@gmail.com

Chapter **1**

OWNING THE STORIES WE TELL
We All Have a Story to Tell

We need to reshape our own perception of how we view ourselves.

We have to step up as women and take the lead.

—Beyoncé

Every time I tuck my six-year-old granddaughter into bed, she asks for the same thing: *Please, Grandma, tell me a real story*. She specifically asks for a "real" story, one that is about me when I was growing up. She knows every neighborhood child by name from 60 years ago, every naughty thing I ever did as a child, and every lesson I learned, all through the ritual of storytelling. Storytelling is my way of passing on knowledge, important teachings, and the collection of my life experiences to my attentive, sleepy yet wide-eyed six-year-old audience.

We all have a story to tell. Our stories connect us to the truths about ourselves, our families, our communities, and our workplaces. This journal is designed to provide the space, forum, and opportunity to pause and reflect on our own stories as we are leading while female. We will recognize ourselves in each other's stories.

In the book, *Leading While Female* (2020), we three authors reached deep into our life experiences to share our stories with each other and the readers. Perhaps most importantly, we wanted to share our stories with ourselves. Through our narratives, we shared fears, hardships, victories, failures, heartaches, jubilation, joy, and love. We learned of our commonalities as well as our unique perspectives and thus our individual contributions to the world.

Many of the stories in this journal, shared with us by our female sisters in leadership, illustrate the power of myths, biases, imposter syndrome, stereotypes, and gender inequities. As we read the stories of others and contemplate our own, this journal provides the counternarrative, a different story for emerging female leaders.

Our stories spark connections and connections build relationships. Relationships make better tomorrows for our children. As we convey our stories today, we hand the baton to future generations so they learn and do better than we have. Now we can all be vulnerable to the process of storytelling and reflecting so that we may learn from each other's life experiences. Within these pages, you will be reading, reflecting, writing, learning, and *leading while female*.

REFLECTIONS

As I reflect on my leadership story, when and where did my story begin?

_____

_____

_____

_____

_____

_____

_____

Who are the main characters in my leadership story?

_____

_____

_____

_____

_____

_____

_____

_____

_____

What crossroads or conflicts have I encountered?

_____

_____

_____

_____

_____

_____

_____

_____

_____

▶ *What happens, though, when stories are written about us before we have a chance to write or even imagine our own story?*

Leading While Female (2020, p. 18)

What story may have been told about you that illustrated stereotypes, myths, biases, or low expectations?

_____

_____

_____

_____

_____

_____

_____

_____

_____

What gender-biased stories have you heard in your lifetime that have contributed to your beliefs and values as a leader?

_____

_____

_____

_____

_____

_____

_____

_____

_____

_____

What might it take for you to be successful in altering the narrative of gender stereotype stories?

_____

_____

_____

_____

_____

_____

_____

_____

_____

_____

_____

_____

_____

_____

_____

_____

_____

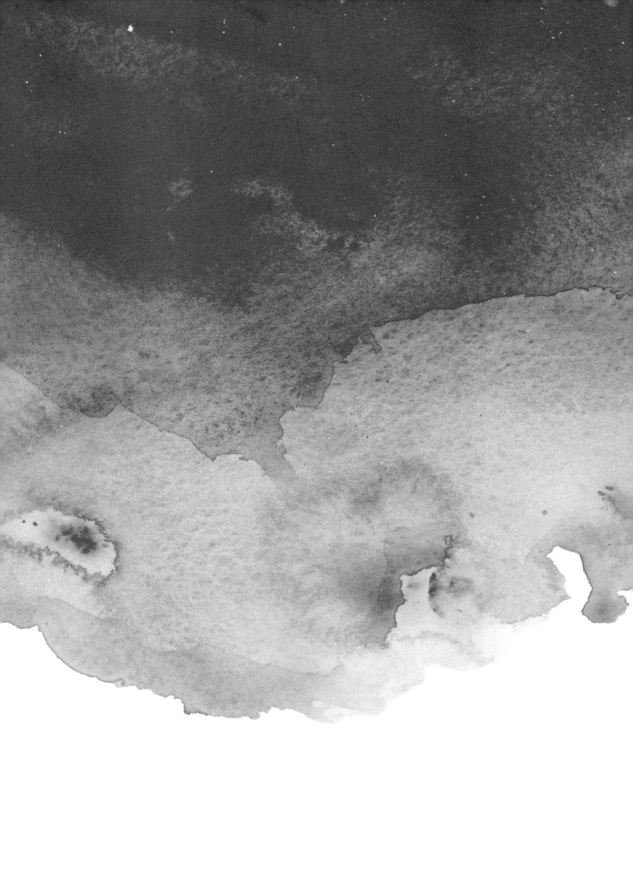

Chapter **2**

CULTURAL PROFICIENCY
A Framework for Gender Equity

Sometimes just being yourself is the radical act. When you occupy spaces in systems that weren't built for you, your authenticity is your activism.

—Elaine Welteroth (2019, p. 200)

I'M LOOKING FOR A PLACE I FEEL I BELONG: ARDA'S STORY

Next time Sara asks me to join her and the group for drinks after work on Friday, I'm going to say, "Yes, I'll be there." Every other time, I've offered some excuse for why I couldn't go. The real reason is I'm a professional and I feel uncomfortable around groups of people who are talking about work and people at work. I like Sara, though. She's different from the other women I work with. At least she has tried to get to know me. Sara is one of several Latinas and I'm the only Armenian American in our division. No one seems interested in who I am or personal things, only what I know and what I do here at work. Yet, everyone knows personal things about each other. I hear them talk about their children and grandchildren. They talk about other family members and travel adventures they have together. I'm never asked about my family or holidays or travel plans. Most of the time, I don't feel like I even belong in this place, although I've worked here for four years as director of assessment and accountability for the County Office of Education. I left my previous district and position because my knowledge and skill level intimidated my supervisor. So, I've been a bit more reserved here than usual. I don't want to intimidate anyone and risk losing my job.

Recently, our department began professional learning about Cultural Proficiency as a leadership practice. One of the strategies caused us to think about ourselves and who we are in relation to others. I thought about my culture. Aspects of my Armenian culture that I'm most proud of are our hospitality, our friendliness, our strong family values, and our kindness and generosity to others. However, I don't feel like I can truly express these aspects of who I am because my colleagues do not know anything about my culture, nor do they seem interested. Maybe if I join Sara and other members of our department for an after-work event, I can engage in enjoying music, food, dancing, talking, and sharing stories of my family and friends. Actually, I'm hoping I've found a workspace where I feel like I belong. I'm not sure what to do. . . .

REFLECTIONS

What might be some barriers Arda is facing as she is leading while female?

_____

_____

_____

_____

_____

Given the story thus far, what might you predict will happen next?

_____

_____

_____

_____

_____

_____

What might be some support factors from which Arda might draw?

_____

_____

_____

_____

_____

_____

What might be some feelings Arda is experiencing?

_____

_____

_____

_____

_____

Describe a time when you experienced a similar situation. What leadership lessons did you learn from that experience?

What else might you like to say as you reflect on Arda's leadership story?

▶ *Discussions of how our country's heritage favored straight, property-owning White men over women and how these inequities (sexism) continue to affect today's schooling are often met with disbelief and dismissed with comments such as,* Women just can't lead like men do.

Leading While Female (2020, p 36)

What's your reaction to the quote? What might your response be to someone who makes that comment?

_____

_____

_____

_____

▶ *The personal exploration of values, beliefs, and assumptions and the intentional review of policies and practices are referred to as the* inside-out process *of culturally proficient educational practice.*

Leading While Female (2020, p. 43)

In what ways is your personal journey representative of the *inside-out process* of Cultural Proficiency?

_____

_____

_____

_____

Chapter **3**

CONFRONTING AND OVERCOMING BARRIERS

The problem with gender is that it prescribes how we should be rather than recognizing how we are. Imagine how much happier we would be, how much freer to be our true selves, if we didn't have the weight of gender expectations.

—Chimamanda Ngozi Adichie (2012, p. 34)

NOW YOU ARE IN CHARGE: CELESTE'S STORY

I reread my contract. I still couldn't believe I got the superintendent job instead of Kirk. I am a newcomer to the district. Kirk was a strong candidate and had been in the district for 10 years; and, after all, he fit the image of former superintendents for the district. Kirk is a tall, straight, White male. As an African American female, I had my work cut out for me to surface as one of three finalists. In addition to Kirk and me, Harland was a finalist for the position. Harland was a very popular "rising star" African American male principal in the district.

Now, in the late afternoon silence of my new office, four weeks into my new role, I examined my contract one more time. Yes, I *am* the new superintendent! The *first* female superintendent in this district. The *first* African American superintendent in this district. I felt an internal smile as I took a long, deep breath and waited for my 5:30 appointment to arrive.

The knock on the door came at precisely 4:58. I knew Amanda would not be late. She was always early. "If you're on time, then you are late. That's what Howard always said," Amanda had said many times. Howard was the former superintendent. Amanda was his administrative assistant. Prior to his retirement, Howard assigned Amanda to another unit as an administrative assistant. He had told me he reassigned her so I would feel comfortable hiring my own administrative assistant. Amanda had let me know she would help me transition to my new role—"That's what Howard would want me to do," she said often.

Our meeting began on a cordial note. Nice greetings were exchanged. I had the hot tea ready to serve. Amanda didn't wait for much chitchat. She started in right away. "You know you are doing some things I told you would make people unhappy. You haven't listened to my advice at all. The school visits you are making have everyone nervous. Howard never did those. Those community meetings are much too early in the year. Howard always waited till the end of the year to have those. He didn't meet with site administrators either. Everything you are doing is micromanaging. Howard never did that!"

And that's how every meeting with Amanda went for the entire first month and a half.

Finally, . . .

REFLECTIONS

What might be some barriers Celeste is facing as she is leading while female?

Given the story thus far, what might you predict will happen next?

What leadership decisions might Celeste make?

What might be some support factors from which Celeste might draw?

What might be some feelings Celeste is experiencing?

Describe a time when you experienced a similar situation. What leadership lessons did you learn from that experience?

What else might you like to say as you reflect on Celeste's leadership story?

▶ *Without careful monitoring by school leaders, gender bias is often embedded and reinforced in textbooks, resources, curriculum, lessons, and the interactions with teachers.*

Leading While Female (2020, p. 56)

In what ways might you assess, monitor, and interrupt culturally destructive instructional practices focused on inequity (including gender inequity)?

What are some lingering stereotypes, biases, and/or misinformation you have encountered along your educational (leadership) journey?

Chapter **4**

MOVING FORWARD WITH GUIDING PRINCIPLES

Women are leaders everywhere you go, from the CEO who runs a Fortune 500 company to the housewife who raises her children and heads her household. Our country was built by strong women, and we will continue to break down walls and defy stereotypes.
—Nancy Pelosi (*Glamour*, 2007)

LOOKING BACK FOR LESSONS LEARNED: RAQUEL'S STORY

I consider myself a woman of principle. My parents worked hard to raise their five children, and we were often reminded that the richness of an individual was found in their character, not in their pocketbooks. I carried that wisdom with me as a teacher and into my new role as a site administrator of a high school.

I frequently found that the guiding principles that guided my life as a woman in leadership were not in alignment with the organizational culture. I was told by my father to not tell him who I was but to show him who I was and then he would tell me my character. Although the guiding principles of the district were clearly articulated and displayed prominently throughout the hallways of our high school, the actual actions of the organization did not often reflect those values. How can people believe what we say when they can clearly see what we do?

Guiding principles such as "We treat all people with dignity and respect" were prominently displayed on posters yet in the staff lounge we spoke disparagingly about families, with accusations that some do not care about the education or success of their children. We minimized homophobic statements and gender disparities.

"We believe in the unique potential of every individual" was another fundamental value of our institution, but we continued to track students in predictable lanes and make it impossible for a student to be in advanced placement courses if they did not have the unearned advantages of financial resources.

"Every person belongs" was so simply stated but was violated with complexities that I experienced daily. I was frequently not looked at in meetings by my male counterparts or dismissed when I had an alternative view. My good ideas were often attributed to a male colleague. Female administrators were expected to fall into the predictable roles of note taker, poster maker, donut supplier, and clean upper at the end of a long meeting. There were times when I thought I did not belong in the organization and considered exiting. I'm pleased and proud to have stayed. I was promoted to principal of the school, and it is now my role to ensure that our actions align with our stated values. Our students are watching. Equity is a lived value, and our students deserve nothing less than the view that we espouse in our guiding principles.

REFLECTIONS

What might be a value that you learned as a young person and are expected to live out within your schools and districts?

_____

_____

_____

_____

What are some of the values that you hold that you may have been asked to leave outside of the school or district?

_____

_____

_____

_____

_____

Assuming that we value gender equity within the educational organization, how will the tools of Cultural Proficiency assist to ensure this value is active?

_____

_____

_____

_____

_____

In what ways do you help others become aware of the core values of the organization?

_____

_____

_____

_____

_____

What might be some conflicting feelings Raquel experienced? Describe a time when you experienced an action within the organization that did not support the stated guiding principles.

_____

_____

_____

_____

_____

_____

_____

_____

_____

_____

_____

_____

_____

What else might you like to say as you reflect on Raquel's leadership story?

_____

_____

_____

_____

_____

_____

_____

_____

_____

▶ *Do our actions reflect our values, and do our values reflect our actions?*

Leading While Female (2020, p. 72)

How might we determine if we really are who we say we are?

_____

_____

_____

_____

_____

_____

_____

_____

_____

How might the organization benefit and thrive from the usage of guiding principles in the support of women as leaders?

_____

_____

_____

_____

_____

_____

_____

_____

_____

_____

Think of a time when you were conflicted in believing what was said because it was contrary to what was being done. What did you notice? How did that make you feel? What might you do in the future to interrupt these behaviors?

_____

_____

_____

_____

_____

_____

_____

_____

_____

_____

_____

_____

_____

_____

_____

Chapter **5**

UNDERSTANDING FEMINISM, IDENTITY, AND INTERSECTIONALITY
Who Am I? Who Are We?

You may encounter many defeats, but you must not be defeated. In fact, it may be necessary to encounter the defeats, so you can know who you are, what you can rise from, how you can still come out of it.

—Maya Angelou

DISCOVERING MY IDENTITY: ANNE'S STORY

For years in my career, I was seen as a rising leader. I was asked to lead efforts to improve student learning and tapped to serve in both informal and formal leadership roles. For so much of that time, I was hesitant. Although many of my peers and family members saw me as successful, the thoughts and voices in my head had tricked me into believing I was less than. I was afraid—afraid that if I shared the very essence of who I am, my credibility would (for no good reason) be ripped away. The internalized oppression—internalized homophobia—led me to believe that I was a disappointment to my family and my faith. It led me to believe I was alone in this world.

Finally, at the age of 28, the day came when I would hide from my family no longer. I remember that day like it was yesterday. My heart raced, then it was like the fog lifted and I could finally see clearly and they could finally see me for who I am. Although things felt somewhat better, I still feared coming out in the workplace. I continued to hide, never sharing milestones like my commitment ceremony, promotions, and other life events with my spouse/partner.

After more than two decades, the time came in my career when I knew I was ready to be a superintendent. I knew there was no way I was going to enter that role without my whole personhood. I knew I needed to "come out" to the board so they never wondered, "What else is she hiding?" Today I stand relieved, able to bring the absolute best of me to work in service to *all* students every day. I have found great empowerment in living my truth. Although I am exhausted with "coming out," stepping out of fear has led to advocacy in my state organization for LGBT (lesbian, gay, bisexual, transgender) students and staff who felt they were only existing in the past. I now realize when executive leaders have a strong sense of their identity, beliefs, and values, they not only free themselves but they are also able to free others through their advocacy. Now, I'm ready to move on to the next steps in my career path. What will it take for me to be a mentor for others? Is it time for me to be an activist?

REFLECTIONS

What might be some barriers Anne has overcome on her journey of leading while female?

_____

_____

_____

_____

_____

Reflecting on the statement, "being able to bring the absolute best of me to work," what might that mean for you in your context of leading while female?

_____

_____

_____

_____

_____

In what ways might personal internalized oppression be affecting your leading-while-female experience?

_____

_____

_____

_____

_____

What aspects of resilience in Anne's story might support your personal journey?

_____

_____

_____

_____

_____

What might be some feelings Anne has experienced?

_____

_____

_____

_____

_____

Describe a time when you experienced a similar situation. What leadership lessons did you learn from that experience?

_____

_____

_____

_____

_____

_____

_____

_____

_____

_____

What might you like to add as you reflect on Anne's leadership story?

_____

_____

_____

_____

_____

_____

▶ *Organizations must clearly understand the* emotional *tax paid on a daily basis when women of color feel they have to be quiet and reserved due to concerns about racial and gender bias.*

Leading While Female (2020, pp. 86–87)

In what ways has the emotional tax impacted you, a friend, or a colleague as a multicultural woman in leadership?

_____

_____

_____

_____

_____

_____

_____

_____

_____

How might these unhealthy experiences impact the organizational success overall?

_____

_____

_____

_____

_____

_____

_____

_____

_____

_____

What might be your next steps to interrupt this barrier?

_____

_____

_____

_____

_____

_____

_____

_____

_____

_____

_____

_____

_____

_____

_____

_____

Chapter **6**

MEN'S ACTIONS AS ALLIES, ADVOCATES, AND MENTORS

Other people can give us the best insight into ourselves—and our own limitations. We must have the courage to ask for help and to request feedback to expand our vision of what's possible.

—Maria Castañón Moats (Macdonald, 2018, p. 14)

I WAS ASSIGNED THE MENTOR FROM HEAVEN: MINH'S STORY

I had been a district leader for more than a decade, yet early in my superintendency tenure, I found myself needing mentorship in a way that I hadn't before. In my previous roles, my mentors showed me the ins and outs of the position or listened with a caring ear as I discussed the many hurdles I was attempting to overcome. This time, rather than having someone to vent to, I knew I needed to seek out someone who had deep experience as a superintendent and who could provide wise counsel related to some tenuous experiences I was having with my board of trustees. I found that I was being questioned on just about every recommendation I took to the board, and this was impacting not only me but my cabinet as well. I had a solid cabinet that was well read and known as experts in their areas of oversight. I knew that their work was aligned with the overall vision I had provided and with our strategic roadmap. Bottom line: The proposals were good for students.

I asked around and heard wonderful things about Bill, so I reached out to him. In our first meeting, he said, "Minh, the first thing to know is that a superintendent needs to understand the thinking of 5–7 supervisors." He encouraged me to stay connected and keep each of them informed—quality relationships were essential. Next, he provided a recipe for garnering quality feedback from stakeholders and getting enough input to propose recommendations that would be moved forward. This was mentoring that stood out differently from simply having a person to run things by. His sage advice and tools of the trade were what I needed to get back on track. Over the years I've learned that *no one mentor is enough*, and that it is all right to have three or four who are known for their expertise in different areas. I also learned that it was okay to enter conversations with a specific ask—if I needed more than a caring listener, I would say that. If I was dealing with a situation where I felt paralyzed, I would say that. It is all right to declare what you are seeking from your mentor(s).

I would be remiss if I didn't talk about my indirect mentoring experiences. When Bill invited me to co-present at conferences, I observed how intentional he is connecting with aspiring and new superintendents and introducing them

(Continued)

(Continued)

to influential leaders. Just as he did with me, he encouraged them to take on roles in the state association.

Now I find myself in the position to mentor those new to the superintendency. It is my time to pay forward the knowledge, time, and wisdom that was given to me. Like Bill, I've come to understand the power of specific intention, and I make certain that educational leaders continue to make room for and prepare aspiring female leaders.

REFLECTIONS

What might be some barriers that Minh faces as she is leading while female?

_____

_____

_____

_____

How might multiple mentors benefit your career aspirations?

_____

_____

_____

_____

Minh references "the power of specific intention." What might this mean to you?

_____

_____

_____

_____

_____

What might be some support factors from Minh's experience that you can draw from?

Describe a time when you experienced a situation similar to Minh's. What leadership lessons did you learn from that experience?

What else might you like to say as you reflect on Minh's leadership story?

▶ *What seems like an unending and winding path toward executive leadership, often requires negotiating unknown situations without the guidance of mentors in the field.*

Leading While Female (2020, p. 85)

What surfaces for you as you reflect on this quote?

_____

_____

_____

_____

_____

_____

_____

_____

How might women leaders position themselves to ensure all women seeking executive leadership roles have a mentor?

_____

_____

_____

_____

_____

_____

_____

_____

_____

What might be your first step in supporting an aspiring female leader?

_____

_____

_____

_____

_____

_____

_____

_____

_____

_____

_____

_____

_____

_____

_____

_____

_____

_____

_____

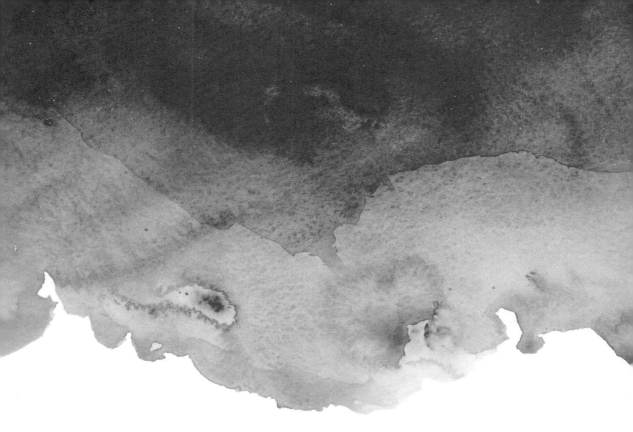

Chapter **7**

NEXT STEPS?

I alone cannot change the world, but I can cast a stone across the water to create many ripples.
—Mother Teresa

MY FIVE-YEAR PLAN TURNED INTO AN EIGHT-YEAR PLAN: KRISTIE'S STORY

When will you know it's time to move to another district or another leadership position? That is the question I have been asked dozens of times by female leaders as they contemplate retirement or moving to another district or position.

As I reflect on my career, I realize my five-year plan turned into an eight-year plan. I had full intentions of leading a small district for my first superintendency. I would learn all I needed to know to prepare me for my next step: a large school district. Well, so much for intentions. I didn't anticipate projects and initiatives that were not on my five-year plan. I didn't anticipate wanting to see the kindergartners through to eighth-grade promotion and I certainly didn't anticipate falling in love with an entire district community.

"What's it like being the first female superintendent in our district?" a board member asked me at the end of my first-year evaluation. As I reflect on that first year, I recall feelings of being challenged on a regular basis to be a woman of confidence and competence. I recall commenting to the board member, "My compassionate, calm, and caring demeanor are not signs of weakness. In fact, they are my greatest strengths." I led the district through some of the most challenging times in the history of our institution—fires, suicides, pandemics, and racial unrest. We came out on the other side as a stronger organization with a deeper resolve to do right by each and every child and their communities. However, by the end of the fifth year, we had not reached the outcomes we had developed through a shared vision process. Our Culturally Proficient Equity Action Plan was incomplete. I realized I needed more time to complete the goals I had set for myself and our district.

How Could I Possibly Leave a District That I Had Grown to Love?

Kristie, you've been a tremendous asset to our district and our community. The words of Myra, president of our board, still resonate for me at the end of Year 7. I had announced the coming year would be my final year in the district. I knew

(Continued)

(Continued)

the time was right for me to transition to another district. I learned there is no designated timeline and no practice districts. The time is right based on personal and professional needs as well as the needs of the district. I recall the exact moment I knew my work was done and the time had come for a new set of eyes, new initiatives, new energy, and a new vision. I also knew it was time for me to move to new challenges and opportunities, not necessarily larger or with higher compensation. What mattered more was my personal and professional growth and the growth of the district.

Leaving was not easy. I cannot minimize the final day as I walked out the door for the last time. I recall thinking issues I had dealt with so intimately were no longer my challenges nor my concerns. I grieved what I had lost, yet the gifts I received helped me smile through the tears. Questions hung over my head: If loving the district changed my life, why am I surprised that leaving the district would also be a life changer? If the district is better because I was there, might it make sense I am better because I was there?

I have moved on to the next district and I find myself in a new organization with new challenges to meet, new opportunities to seize, and new relationships to build. I find myself falling in love again. This may be my last district . . . or not. I will know when it is time for me. I will know when it is time for the organization. In the meantime, I am right where I am meant to be.

REFLECTIONS

What are some unique challenges to knowing when it is time for a change as you are leading while female?

_____

_____

_____

_____

_____

What timelines have you set for yourself in your career that did not go as planned?

In what ways are the roles of competence and confidence important as you make decisions to move within or outside of your current district?

What will you do when you are done with your professional career? What lessons and skills that you learned while leading might you take with you into your next chapter of life?

Describe a time when you experienced a moment that spoke to you and impacted your life trajectory.

_____

_____

_____

_____

_____

_____

_____

_____

_____

_____

_____

_____

_____

What else might you like to say as you reflect on Kristie's leadership story?

_____

_____

_____

_____

_____

_____

_____

_____

_____

_____

_____

▶ *Now is the time for females to lead and take action that is inclusive of their mentors, male and female, for gender equity in educational leadership.*

Leading While Female (2020, p. 100)

What are the key actions that you are willing to commit toward gender equity within your organization?

_____

_____

_____

_____

_____

_____

_____

_____

_____

_____

Who is mentoring you . . . and who are you mentoring?

_____

_____

_____

_____

_____

_____

_____

_____

_____

_____

_____

The authors dedicated the book to their mothers. To whom do you dedicate your work as you lead while female?

_____

_____

_____

_____

_____

_____

_____

_____

_____

_____

_____

_____

_____

_____

_____

_____

_____

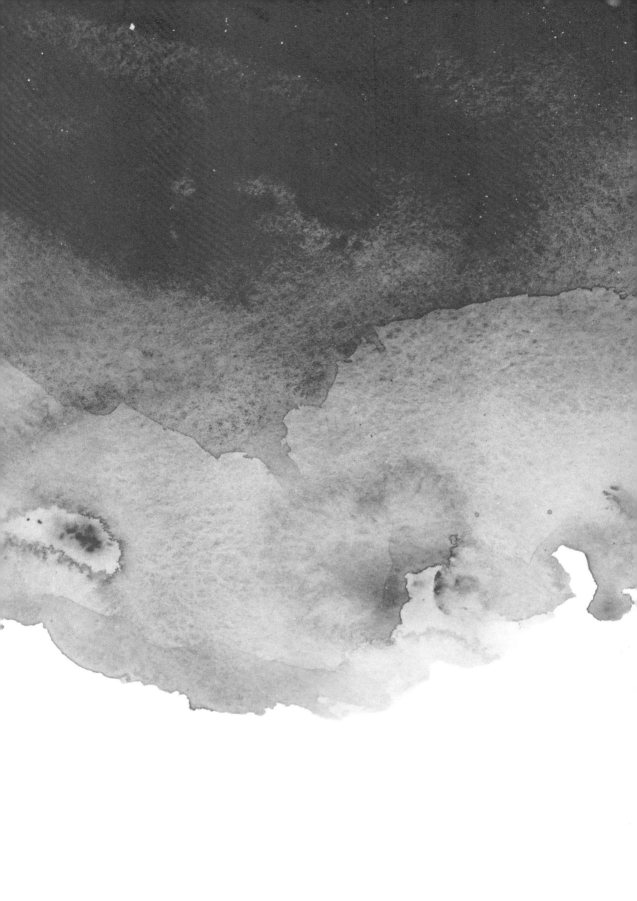

Chapter 8

PAYING IT FORWARD

Do not follow where the path may lead.

Go instead where there is no path and leave a trail.

—Muriel Strode (1903, p. 505)

I'M RETIRING FROM INSTITUTIONS, NOT FROM THE PROFESSION: ROSARIO'S STORY

We were leaving in a few minutes for a two-week vacation. I couldn't believe it. Really? Tomas and I had not taken time away on a non–work-related trip in several years. We had both retired from our full-time positions two years earlier. I had served for seven years as a local superintendent, and Tomas had been a university professor for 25 years.

He had enjoyed supporting his students through their dissertation process for the past five years but had decided to retire because of complications related to hip surgery. We coordinated our retirement schedules for the same month of the same year. Everything seemed like such a great plan until several emerging female leaders from my former district asked me if I would mentor them through their career planning as part of a new Women in Education Leadership (WEL) organization. I was also surprised when one of the directors contacted me and asked if I would serve on the board of directors of WEL. I said yes without really knowing what would be required of me. I thought I'd enjoy working with young female leaders. Little did I know, my email inbox would soon be filled with requests to mentor female leaders as principals, doctoral students, directors, and superintendents.

"Ready to go, Ros?" my husband yelled upstairs. "We need to get on the road soon. Traffic, you know!" Ok, I needed to respond to a few more emails before we left for our trip. Each message was a plea for my time and energy to coach, advise, mentor, or guide a possible mentee for the upcoming year. Could I meet for coffee, for lunch, for dinner, or even virtually? These young women seemed desperate for another female to walk this journey with them. I read stories about unsupportive spouses, uncooperative supervisors, uneasy candidates, and those unwilling to leave their district. I found myself saying, "Yes, here's my cell #. Let's talk soon."

I find this unpaid work to be very rewarding. I'm meeting remarkable women. I've also attended professional learning sessions to become a better coach and mentor. This is important work. I often find myself exhausted and at the same time, these opportunities bring me joy. A friend from my former district, who I had not seen for over a year, called and invited me to go to lunch.

(Continued)

(Continued)

She said, "Now that you are retired, I know you have plenty of time. So, you pick a convenient time for you." I responded, "Well, Susan, I retired from the institution, but not from the profession. I'm busy giving back to young women who are finding their way through the system."

I'm wondering who else I might invite to join me in this work. I'm exhausted—in a good way.

REFLECTIONS

What are some unique rewards you look forward to as you are leading while female?

_____

_____

_____

_____

What might be some plans you are making toward your retirement as your career develops?

_____

_____

_____

_____

_____

In what ways might you support/coach/mentor other female leaders as you are leading while female?

_____

_____

_____

_____

_____

Describe a time when your leadership experience/story might impact an emerging leader. What lessons might you share?

_____

_____

_____

_____

_____

_____

_____

_____

_____

_____

_____

_____

What else might you like to say as you reflect on Rosario's leadership story?

_____

_____

_____

_____

_____

_____

_____

_____

_____

_____

▶ *Now that you know what you know about gender inequities and imbalances in educational leadership, to what actions are you willing to commit?*

Leading While Female (2020, p. 100)

What might be some things about gender inequities and imbalances that have impacted your career path thus far or the career paths of women leaders you've observed?

_____

_____

_____

_____

_____

_____

_____

_____

_____

_____

What have been your reactions to those inequities and imbalances you've experienced or observed?

_____

_____

_____

_____

_____

_____

_____

_____

_____

_____

_____

What actions might you take to interrupt these inequities for female leaders?

_____

_____

_____

_____

_____

_____

_____

_____

_____

_____

_____

_____

_____

_____

_____

_____

Chapter **9**

TEMPLATE FOR ACTION
My Stormy First Draft (SFD)

Own your story and you get to write the ending.

Deny the story and it owns you.

—Brené Brown (2018, p. 270)

Your stormy first Draft (SFD) is the story you are making up about yourself. Brené Brown calls it the myth making that's going on in your head. Story writing is one way to grab hold of that mess before it takes complete hold of you (Brown, 2018). Once you've written your SFD, you can own it and then rewrite your current reality and your desired state.

Here is your opportunity to write your SFD. Take a deep breath. Relax. Breathe. Relax. Think. Feel. Write.

SFD . . . This is the leadership story I'm making up: What's getting in the way of my future story?

As I think of this story, the emotions I feel are

My body's reactions are

My best thinking about my story right now is

_____

_____

_____

_____

_____

Currently, my beliefs about leading are

_____

_____

_____

_____

_____

Currently, my values about leading are

_____

_____

_____

_____

_____

My assumptions about leading while female and gender (in)equity are

_____

_____

_____

_____

_____

Therefore, when I face challenges, my actions typically include

_____

_____

_____

_____

_____

In what ways are these actions aligned with my values, current beliefs, and assumptions?

_____

_____

_____

_____

_____

Now that I own my story, what do I need to know and do to write my new story?

_____

_____

_____

_____

_____

Some key elements of my new story are

_____

_____

_____

_____

_____

Who else might be supportive of my new story?

_____

_____

_____

_____

_____

_____

_____

_____

_____

Now, what action might I take, who might I mentor, and what decision needs to be made for me to own my new leadership story?

_____

_____

_____

_____

_____

_____

_____

_____

_____

_____

_____

_____

_____

_____

MY LEADERSHIP STORY: (TITLE)_____

REFERENCES

Adichie, Chimamanda Ngozi. (2012). *We should all be feminists*. Anchor Books.

Arriaga, Trudy, Stanley, Stacie, & Lindsey, Delores. (2020). *Leading while female: A culturally proficient response for gender equity*. Corwin.

Brown, Brené. (2018). *Dare to lead: Brave work. Tough conversations. Whole hearts.* Vermilion.

Glamour. (2007, November 4). Nancy Pelosi: Women of the year 2007. *Glamour magazine.* https://www.glamour.com/story/nancy-pelosi

Macdonald, Lylette. (2018). More than words from women in BICSI: My journey through ICT convergence. *BICSI, 6*(1), 13–14.

Strode, Muriel. (1903, August). Wind-wafted wild flowers. *The Open Court, 17*(8), 505.

Welteroth, Elaine. (2019). *More than enough: Claiming space for who you are (no matter what they say)*. Penguin Books.

CORWIN

A SAGE Publishing Company

Helping educators make the greatest impact

CORWIN HAS ONE MISSION: to enhance education through intentional professional learning.

We build long-term relationships with our authors, educators, clients, and associations who partner with us to develop and continuously improve the best evidence-based practices that establish and support lifelong learning.

Continue Learning

Consultants for Cultural Proficiency and Women in Leadership, offering facilitation of:

- Book studies
- Leadership retreats for female executives
- Onsite keynotes, presentations, and multiple day trainings
- Actions for equity planning and implementing

Trudy T. Arriaga
805-766-3377

Stacie L. Stanley
651-387-7589

Delores B. Lindsey,
The Lindsey Group LLC
www.ccpep.org
714-366-7561

EQ22108553

CORWIN